Money and Success

LIFE ON THE EDGE SERIES

Money and Success

Dr. James Dobson

WORD PUBLISHING

NASHVILLE

A Thomas Nelson Company

MONEY AND SUCCESS

PUBLISHED BY WORD PUBLISHING, NASHVILLE, TENNESSEE.

© 2000 by James Dobson. All rights reserved. No portion of this book may be reproduced, stored in a retrieval system, or transmitted in any form or by any means—electronic, mechanical, photocopy, recording, or any other—except for brief quotations in printed reviews, without the prior permission of the publisher.

Unless otherwise indicated, Scripture quotations used in this book are from The Holy Bible, New International Version (NIV). Copyright © 1973, 1978, 1984, International Bible Society. Used by permission of Zondervan Bible Publishers.

Other references are from the following source:
The King James Version of the Bible (KJV).

LIBRARY OF CONGRESS CATALOGING-IN-PUBLICATION DATA

Dobson, James C., 1936–
     Money and success / by James Dobson.
          p. cm. — (Life on the edge series)
     ISBN 0-8499-4228-4
          1. Young adults—Religious life. 2. Money—Religious aspects—
Christianity. 3. Success—Religious aspects—Christianity. I. Title.
BV4529.2 .D63 2001
241'.68—dc21
                                                                        00-049968
                                                                              CIP

Printed in the United States of America.

00 01 02 03 04 05 PHX 9 8 7 6 5 4 3 2 1

Preface

IF YOU ARE BETWEEN SIXTEEN AND TWENTY-SIX years of age, this series of books is written specifically for you. Others are welcome to read along with us, of course, but the ideas are aimed directly at those moving through what we will call the "critical decade."

Some of the most dramatic and permanent changes in life usually occur during those ten short years. A person is transformed from a kid who's still living at home and eating at the parents' table to a full-fledged adult who should be earning a living and taking complete charge of his or her life. Most of the decisions that will shape the next fifty years will be made in this era, including the choice of an occupation, perhaps the decision to marry, and the establishment of values and principles by which life will be governed.

I recall pondering these questions in my youth and thinking how helpful it would be to talk with someone who had a few answers—someone who understood what I was facing. But like most of my friends, I never asked for help.

What makes this period even more significant is the impact of early mistakes and errors in judgment. They can undermine all that is to follow. A bricklayer knows he must be very careful to get his foundation absolutely straight; any wobble in the bricks at the bottom will create an even greater tilt as the wall goes up. So it is in life.

In this series of books, we'll talk about how to interpret the will of God and recognize His purposes for you, the task of thinking through the challenges you are facing, and how you will accomplish your life goals. A contractor would never begin a skyscraper without detailed architectural and engineering plans to guide his or her work. Likewise, persons in the critical decade between age sixteen and twenty-six owe it to their future to figure out who they are and what they want out of life. Helping you do that is what this book is all about.

—Dr. James Dobson

Introduction

*"But seek ye first the kingdom of God, and His righ-
teousness; and all these things shall be added unto you."*
— Matthew 6:33 KJV

AT SOME POINT IN YOUR LIFE, YOU WILL HAVE TO
answer the following question: Do I pursue earthly or
eternal success?

The answer you give to that question will have
tremendous consequences for your life.

The temptation to pursue power and money can
be a hard one to resist. If we choose to frantically
chase these goals, believing they will lead us down the
road to happiness, we are bound to be disappointed.
As the years pass, we will discover that neither one
can satisfy the emptiness that is deep down inside us.
King Solomon came to this realization when he
wrote in the book of Ecclesiastes: "Whoever loves
money never has money enough; whoever loves

wealth is never satisfied with his income. This too is meaningless" (Ecclesiastes 5:10 NIV).

The path of eternal success, however, will fill that emptiness and provide you with a satisfaction that will not come from material wealth. In *Money and Success,* Dr. James Dobson will show you how you can avoid the pitfall of pursuing earthly treasure and how you can develop an eternal perspective that will provide you with peace, hope, and happiness.

Contents

1   The Money Treadmill

I SAT IN THE INTERNATIONAL AIRPORT IN Atlanta, Georgia, eating a fat-free yogurt and watching all the busy people rushing to and fro. Fascinating little dramas were played out before me. A mother scurried past on her way to gate 92. Trailing far behind her was a toddler who couldn't care less about catching their plane. He was singing little songs and dawdling happily through the terminal. Mom finally turned around and tried to speed him up. No chance! As they disappeared into the crowd, he was ten feet behind his mama and still losing ground.

Then came a maintenance man en route to a broken pipe or a blown circuit. He wore a yellow rubber apron on which he had written the name "Whippie." I wondered how he got that nickname and why he wanted the world to know about it. If you're out there, Whippie—I noticed!

A teenage girl and her mother then walked by. They looked like they had been in a big fight earlier that morning. Maybe it was the girl's weird hairdo that had set them on edge. Whatever started the battle, the kid had apparently won it. Mom was pretty haggard for so early in the day. The adolescent had obviously spent hours that morning trying to make herself look sexy and older than her years. She had succeeded. Hang in there, Mom!

Life in the fast lane is coming your way. I guarantee it.

Hundreds of other people hurried past my observation post before I finished the yogurt. All of them were deep in thought—intent on getting somewhere quick and doing whatever they came to do. I couldn't help wondering who these human beings were and what concerns they carried this day. Back in the 1960s, the Beatles rock group sang about "all the lonely people," asking "where do they all come from?"[1] Yes, I saw a few folks who looked like they desperately needed a friend. But mostly, I saw busy, exhausted men and women who appeared to be hours behind schedule. Would it really have created an international crisis if they had pulled up a chair beside me and watched the people go by for a few minutes? I know! I know! Planes don't wait.

What I witnessed in the Atlanta airport is characteristic of the modern way of doing things. You may not yet be caught up in it, having so recently enjoyed the carefree days of adolescence. But life in the fast lane is coming your way. I guarantee it. The frantic pace of living that almost deprives us of meaning is very contagious, and most people find themselves on its treadmill sooner or later.

The frantic pace of living that almost deprives us of meaning is very contagious.

2 | Life's Really Big Questions

IT IS SO IMPORTANT TO PAUSE AND THINK through some basic issues while you are young, before the pressures of job and family become distracting. There are several eternal questions everyone must deal with eventually. You will benefit, I think, from doing that work now.

Whether you are an atheist, a Muslim, a Buddhist, a Jew, a New-Ager, an agnostic, or a Christian, the questions confronting the human family are the same. Only the answers will differ. They are:

Who am I as a person?

How did I get here?

What really matters to me?

Is Someone keeping score?

What does He expect of me?

Is there life after death?

How do I achieve eternal life, if it exists?

What is the meaning of death?

And then there is one other question that is foundational: What goals are worthy of the investment of my life? These should be resolved before pressing any further into adulthood.

GAME-SHOW GREED

When it comes to purposes and goals, most people appear motivated primarily by the pursuit of money and the things it can buy. If you doubt that, turn on daytime television and watch the contestants as they compete for prizes and cash. Observe the cuckoo birds as they leap in the air, frothing at the mouth and tearing at the clothes of the host. Notice that their eyes are dilated and their ears are bright pink. It's a condition known as *game-show greed,* and it renders its victims incapable of rational judgment.

Yes, BETTY MOLINO, YOU have won a NEW WASH-ING MACHINE, a year's supply of CHEWY CANDY BARS, and this marvelous new doll, WANDA WEE-WEE, that actually soaks your daughter's lap! CON-GRATULATIONS, BETTY, and thanks for playing "GRAB BAG" (frantic applause).

How do I know so much about game-show greed? Because I've been there! Back in 1967, my lovely wife managed to drag me to the *Let's Make a Deal* show, which was the rage at that time. Shirley put toy birds all over her head and blouse, and I carried a dumb sign that said, "My wife is for the birds." Really funny, huh? It was good enough to get the host, Monty Hall, to choose us as lucky contestants. The producers placed us in the two front seats near the cameras but began the program by "dealing" with other suckers.

I kept thinking as I sat there in contestants' row, *What in the world am I doing here holding this stupid sign?* I couldn't have been more skeptical about the proposition. Finally, Monty called our names, and the cameras zoomed in.

> *What goals are worthy of the investment of my life?*

"Here behind door number one is . . . *(a curtain opens)* . . . A NEEEEW CAAR!!" *(The audience goes crazy with excitement.)*

Suddenly, I was gripped by a spasm in the pit of my stomach. My mouth watered profusely, and my heart began knocking on the sides of my chest. There on that stage was the car of my dreams—a brand-new Camaro. Desire came charging up my throat

7

and stuck in the region on my Adam's apple. My breathing became irregular and shallow, which was another unmistakable clue that I had been struck by game-show greed.

To understand this reaction, you would have to know that I have owned several of the worst cars in automotive history. Throughout my college years I drove a 1949 Mercury convertible (I called it Ol' Red) that had power seats, power windows, power top, power everything—but no power to run them. I put the windows up in the winter and down in the summer. There they remained, despite fluctuating temperatures. Shirley, who was then my girlfriend, must have loved me tremendously to have put up with that car. She *hated* it! The front seat had a spring with a bad temper that tore her clothes and punctured her skin. Nor did Ol' Red always choose to run. Every few days, Shirley and I would take this junk heap out for a push.

We both experienced incredible greed, and the feeling was not comfortable.

WHY I WANTED THAT NEW CAR

The crowning blow occurred shortly after our graduation from college. We were invited to appear for important job interviews, and we put on our Sunday best for the occasion. There we were, suit and tie, heels and hose, going sixty miles an hour down the road in Ol' Red, when the convertible top suddenly blew off. Strings and dust flapped us in the face as the canvas waved behind the car like Superman's cape. The ribs of the top protruded above our heads, reminiscent of undersized roll-over bars. It was very embarrassing. And can you believe that Shirley got mad at *me* for letting that happen? She crouched on the floorboard, blaming me for driving such a beat-up car. It is a miracle that our relationship survived that emotional afternoon.

Although Ol' Red had been put to sleep long before our appearance on *Let's Make a Deal,* I still had never owned a new car. Every available dollar had been allocated for tuition in graduate school. I had finished my Ph.D. just two months earlier.

This explains my reaction to the beautiful automobile behind door number one.

"All you have to do to win the car," said Monty, "is tell us the prices of four items."

Shirley and I guessed the first three but blew it on number four. "Sorry," said Monty. "You've been zonked. But here, take a vacuum cleaner and three dollars. And thanks for playing *Let's Make a Deal!*

Shirley and I were just sick. On the way home we talked about how our emotions had been manipulated in that situation. We both experienced incredible greed, and the feeling was not comfortable. I have since learned a very valuable lesson about lust and how it operates in a spiritual context. It has been my observation that whatever a person hungers for, Satan will appear to offer in exchange for a spiritual compromise. In my case, a new automobile was the perfect enticement to unleash my greed. If illicit sex is your desire, it will eventually be made available. Don't be surprised when you are beckoned by a willing partner.

Satan uses our keenest appetites to tempt us.

If your passion is for fame or power, that object of lust will be promised (even if never delivered).

Remember that Jesus was offered bread following His forty-day fast in the wilderness. He was promised power and glory after He had been contemplating His upcoming road to the cross. My point is that Satan uses our keenest appetites to tempt us.

3 Watch Out! Temptation Ahead!

IF YOU HUNGER AND THIRST FOR GREAT wealth—beware! You are in a very precarious position. If you doubt it, look at 1 Timothy 6:9, which says, "People who want to get rich fall into temptation and a trap and into many foolish and harmful desires that plunge men into ruin and destruction." What incredible insight into the nature of mankind. If you watch people who care passionately about money, you'll observe that many of them are suckers for wild-eyed schemes and shady deals. They are always on the verge of a bonanza that seems to slip through their fingers. Instead of getting rich, they just get taken.

Billionaire John D. Rockefeller had some cogent advice for those who wanted to be rich. "It's easy," he said. "All you have to do is get up early, work hard— and strike oil." Easy for him to say.

This discussion reminds me of a deer-hunting trip I took with my son when he was a teenager. We got into the stand very early in the morning before the sun came up. About twenty yards away from us was a feeder that operated on a timer. At 7:00 A.M. it automatically dropped kernels of corn into a pan below.

Ryan and I huddled together in this stand, talking softly about whatever came to mind. Then, through the fog, we saw a beautiful doe emerge silently into the clearing. She took nearly thirty minutes to get to the feeder near where we were hiding. We had no intention of shooting her, but it was fun to watch this beautiful animal from close range. She was extremely wary, sniffing the air and listening for the sounds of danger. Finally, she inched her way to the feeder, still looking around skittishly as though sensing our presence. Then she ate a quick breakfast and fled.

I whispered to Ryan, "There is something valuable to be learned from what we have just seen. Whenever you come upon a free supply of high-quality corn, provided unexpectedly right there in the middle of the forest, be careful! The people who put it there are

> *Through the fog, we saw a beautiful doe emerge silently into the clearing.*

probably sitting nearby in a stand, just waiting to take a shot at you. Keep your eyes and ears open!"

> *God is entitled to a portion of our income—not because He needs it but because we need to give it.*
>
> *Thirty-eight Values to Live By*
> —Dr. James Dobson

Ryan may not always remember that advice, but I will. It isn't often that a father says something to his teenage son that he considers to be profound. And it has applicability to you. The greedier you become, the more vulnerable you are to the con men of our time. They will bait the trap with high-quality "corn," whether it be money, sex, an attractive job offer, or flattery. You'll hardly be able to believe your eyes. What a deal! But take care! Your pretty head may already be in the scope of some-one's rifle.

Not only are there pitfalls for those who seek riches, but the few who acquire them are in for a disappointment. They quickly learn that wealth will not

LIFE ON THE EDGE

satisfy their need for significance. No amount of money will do that.

A popular bumper sticker reads, "He who dies with the most toys, wins." It's a lie. It should read, "He who dies with the most toys, dies anyway." I hope you will believe me when I say that a lifetime invested in the accumulation of things will have been wasted. There *has* to be a better reason for living than that.

4 | Money: Jesus' Most Talked-About Topic

HAVE YOU EVER WONDERED WHAT TOPIC JESUS talked about more often than any other? Was it heaven, hell, sin, repentance, love, or His second coming? No, it was money, and most of what He said came in the form of a warning. This caution about possessions and riches appeared throughout Jesus' teachings. Here are a few passages just from one of the four Gospels, the book of Luke:

Jesus said to a crowd of His followers, "But woe to you who are rich, for you have already received your comfort" (Luke 6:24).

He also said, "Watch out! Be on your guard against all kinds of greed; a man's life does not consist in the abundance of his possessions" (Luke 12:15).

Jesus told a parable about a rich fool who had no need of God. The man believed he had many years to live and said to himself, "'You have plenty of good things laid up for many years. Take life easy; eat, drink and be merry.' But God said to him, 'You fool! This very night your life will be demanded from you. Then who will get what you have prepared for yourself?'" Jesus ended the parable with this sober warning: "This is how it will be with anyone who stores up things for himself but is not rich toward God" (Luke 12:18–21).

> *"For what shall it profit a man if he shall gain the whole world, and lose his own soul?" (Jesus' words in Mark 8:36 KJV).*
>
> *Thirty-eight Values to Live By*
> —Dr. James Dobson

Jesus later visited the home of a prominent Pharisee and said to His host, "When you give a luncheon or dinner, do not invite your friends, your brothers or relatives, or your rich neighbors; if you do, they may invite you back and so you will be repaid. But when you give a banquet, invite the poor, the crippled, the lame, the blind, and you will be blessed" (Luke 14:12–14).

He told a parable of the prodigal son who demanded his inheritance early and then squandered it on prostitutes and riotous living (see Luke 15:11–31).

Jesus said to His disciples, "No servant can serve two masters. Either he will hate the one and love the other, or he will be devoted to the one and despise the other. You cannot serve both God and Money" (Luke 16:13).

He told a parable of the rich man who had everything. The man was clothed in fine purple and linen, and he ate the very best food. But he was unconcerned about the misery of the beggar Lazarus, who was hungry and covered with sores. The rich man died and went to hell where he was tormented, but Lazarus was taken to heaven where he was comforted (see Luke 16:19).

He spoke to a rich young ruler and commanded him to sell all he had and give it to the poor. The man went away very sorrowfully "because he was a man of great wealth" (Luke 18:18–23).

Finally, Jesus turned to His disciples and said, "How hard it is for the rich to enter the kingdom of God! Indeed, it is easier for a camel to go through the eye of a needle than for a rich man to enter the kingdom of God" (Luke 18:24).

Isn't it incredible how many of Jesus' statements dealt with money in one way or another? We must ask ourselves why. Is there a reason the Master kept returning to that theme? Of course there is. Jesus was teaching us that great spiritual danger accompanies the pursuit and the achievement of wealth. He explained why in Matthew 6:21: "For where your treasure is, there your heart will be also."

GIVE THE LORD FIRST PLACE

In *Finding God's Will for Your Life* I wrote: The mission sometimes fails because an individual refuses to include God in his lofty plans. The psalmist wrote, "Except the Lord build the house, they labour in vain that build it: except the Lord keep the city, the watchman waketh but in vain" (Ps. 127:1 KJV). Those words offer incredible meaning for those of you who are just getting started in life. Whatever you try to do, whether it is to build or defend, will be useless if you do it in your own strength. That may sound very old fashioned, but I promise you it is true.

The Lord will not settle for second place in your life. That is the threat posed by money. It can become our treasure—our passion—our greatest love. And when that happens, God becomes almost irrelevant.

Now, what does this understanding mean in today's world? Are we prohibited from earning a living, owning a home and car, having a savings account? Certainly not. In fact, we read in 1 Timothy 5:8, "If anyone does not provide for his relatives, and especially for his immediate family, he has denied the faith and is worse than an unbeliever." Men, specifically, are required to provide for and protect their families, which requires them to bring in money from their labors.

Wealth is not an evil in itself, either. Abraham, David, and other great men of the Bible were blessed with riches. And in fact, the Scriptures indicate that God

Money is not the problem. It is the love of money that is the root of all evil (see 1 Tim. 6:10).

gives to some people the power to get wealth (see Deut. 8:18 and 1 Sam. 2:7). Then where is the point of danger? The apostle Paul clarified for us that money is not the problem. It is the love of money that is the root of all evil (see 1 Tim. 6:10). We get into trouble when our possessions become a god to us.

What, then, is the biblical approach to possessions and money? We've seen what is wrong, but what is right? According to Christian financial counselor and author Ron Blue, there are four principles for money management that are foundational. If

19

they are implemented in your life, you'll never have a problem with materialism. Let's look at them quickly:

Principle 1. God owns it all.

Some people have the notion that the Lord is entitled to 10 percent of our income, which is called our "tithes," and that the other 90 percent belongs to us. Not true. I believe strongly in the concept of tithing, but not because God's portion is limited to a tenth. We are but stewards of all that He has entrusted to us. He is our possessor—and sometimes our dispossessor. Everything we have is but a loan from Him. When God took away his wealth, Job had the correct attitude, saying, "'Naked I came from my mother's womb, and naked I will depart.' The Lord gave and the Lord has taken away; may the name of the Lord be praised" (Job 1:21).

If you understand this basic concept, it becomes clear that every spending decision is a spiritual decision. Waste, for example, is not a squandering of our resources. It is a poor use of His.

Expenditures for worthwhile purposes, such as vacations, ice cream, bicycles, blue jeans, magazines, tennis rackets, cars, and hamburgers, are also purchased with His money. That's why in my family, we bow to thank the Lord before eating each meal. Everything, including our food, is a gift from His hand.

Principle 2. There is always a trade-off between time and effort and money and rewards.

You've heard the phrases "There's no such thing as a free lunch," and "You can't get something for nothing." Those are very important understandings. Money should always be thought of as linked to work and the sweat of our brow.

Here's how this second principle has meaning for us. Think for a moment of the most worthless, unnecessary purchase you have made in recent years. Perhaps it was an electric shaver that now sits in the garage, or an article of clothing that will never be worn. It is important to realize that this item was not purchased with your money; it was bought with your time, which you traded for money. In effect, you swapped a certain proportion of your allotted days on earth for that piece of junk that now clutters your home.

When you understand that everything you buy is purchased with a portion of your life, it should make you more careful with the use of money.

Principle 3. There is no such thing as an independent financial decision.

There will never be enough money for everything you'd like to buy or do. Even billionaires have some limitations on their purchasing power. Therefore, every expenditure has implications for other things you need or want. It's all linked together. What this means is that those who can't resist blowing their money for junk are limiting themselves in areas of greater need or interest.

And by the way, husbands and wives often fight over the use of money. Why? Because their value systems differ and they often disagree on what is wasteful. My mother and father were typical in this regard. If Dad spent five dollars for shotgun shells or for tennis balls, he justified the expenditure because it brought him pleasure. But if Mom bought a five-dollar potato peeler that wouldn't work, he considered that wasteful. Never mind the fact that she enjoyed shopping as much as he did hunting or playing tennis. Their perspectives were simply unique. This is a potential problem you and your future spouse will just have to work through.

Again, this third principle involves a recognition that an extravagance at one point will eventually lead to frustration at another point. Good business managers are able to keep the big picture in mind as they make their financial decisions.

Principle 4. Delayed gratification is the key to financial maturity.

Since we have limited resources and unlimited choices, the only way to get ahead financially is to deny ourselves some of the things we want. If we don't have the discipline to do that, then we will always be in debt. Remember too that unless you spend less than you earn, no amount of income will be enough. That's why some people receive salary increases and soon find themselves even deeper in debt.

Let me repeat that important concept: No amount of income will be sufficient if spending is not brought under control. Consider the finances of the United States government, for example. It extracts more than a trillion dollars annually from American taxpayers. That's a thousand billion bucks! But our Congress spends hundreds of billions more than that.

Even by the most liberal interpretation, much of this revenue is wasted on programs that don't work and on unnecessary and expensive bureaucracies. Consequently, the size of our national debt is mind-boggling. The point is inescapable: Whether it be within a government or by a private individual, there must be a willingness to deny short-term gratification and to live within one's means. It isn't easy, but it pays big dividends at maturity.[2]

A SOLID FINANCIAL FOUNDATION

Well, maybe these four principles will help you build a foundation of financial stability without compromising your belief system. In short, the secret of successful living is to spend your life on something that will outlast it, or, as the writer to the Hebrews said, "Keep your lives free from the love of money and be content with what you have" (Heb. 13:5).

Let's return to the question with which we began: What goals are worthy of the investment of your life? We haven't answered it definitively, but we've eliminated money as a worthy objective. We'll look at another alternative in the next chapter.

5   The Pursuit of Power

WE HAVE BEEN TALKING ABOUT THE BASIC motivators of human behavior and how they relate to the choices that must be made during the critical decade. One of them, the pursuit of money, has been discredited (I hope) as a valid reason for living. Now we will look at another driving force that is even more influential in shaping the way things work. I'm referring to the pursuit of power. The lust for it permeates human societies and has its origins very early in life.

A child between eighteen and thirty-six months of age is a skilled powerbroker. He or she loves to run things—and break things, squash things, flush things, and eat horrible things. Comedian Bill Cosby once said, "Give me 200 active two-year-olds, and I could conquer the world." It's true. Toddlers, in their cute, charming way, can be terrors. They honestly believe the universe revolves around them, and they like it that way.

I remember a three-year-old who was sitting on the potty when a huge earthquake shook the city of Los Angeles. Dishes were crashing and furniture was skidding across the floor. The little boy hung on to his potty-chair and said to his mother, "What did I do, Mom?" It was a logical question from his point of view. If something important had happened, he must have been responsible for it.

> *"The love of money is the root of all evil" (1 Tim. 6:10 KJV). That's why Jesus issues more warnings about materialism and wealth than any other sin. Obviously, it takes a steady hand to hold a full cup.*
>
> *Thirty-eight Values to Live By*
> —Dr. James Dobson

This heady confidence lasts but a few short years, as we have seen. It gives way to self-doubt and insecurity. Alas, one of the most uncomfortable features of adolescence is the sense of powerlessness it can bring. One mother told me that her seventh-grade daughter was getting ridiculed at school every day. She said the girl awakened an hour before she had to get up each morning and lay there thinking about how she could get through her day without being humiliated. Millions of teenagers could identify with her.

Other adolescents resent the fact that their parents hold all the power. As minors, they can't vote, drive, drink, have sex, or run their own lives—unless they break the rules. Some of them resent that situation and refuse to accept it. This leads to the rebellion with which we are all familiar. It is an early grab for power instead of waiting to inherit it naturally in the twenties. Some tragic mistakes are often made by those who acquire the reins of control before their maturity is adequate to handle it.

POWER AND ADOLESCENT RELATIONSHIPS

It is impossible to understand adolescent society without comprehending the role of power in interpersonal relationships. You have recently been there and should be able to recall that competitive environment. That is the heart and soul of its value system. It comes in various forms, of course. For girls, there is no greater social dominance than physical beauty. A truly gorgeous young woman is so powerful that even the boys are often afraid of her. She rules in a high-school setting

27

like a queen on a throne, and in fact, she is usually granted a title with references to royalty in its name (Homecoming Queen, All-School Queen, Sweetheart Queen, Football Queen, Prom Queen, etc.). The way she uses that status with her peers is fascinating to those of us who are interested in human behavior.

For boys, power games are much more physical than for girls. The bullies literally cram their will down the throats of those who are weaker. That is what I remember from my own high-school years. I had a number of fights during that era just to defend my turf. There was one guy, however, whom I had no intention of tackling. His name was McKeechern, but we called him Killer. He was the terror of the town. Everyone believed Killer would dismantle anyone who crossed him. That theory was never tested to my knowledge. At least, not until I blundered into a confrontation.

When I was fifteen years old and an impulsive sophomore, I nearly ended a long and happy manhood before it had a chance to get started. As I recall, a blizzard had blown through our state the night before and a group of us had gathered in front of the school to throw snowballs at passing cars. (Does that tell you anything about our collective maturity at the time?) Just before the afternoon bell rang, I looked up the street and saw McKeechern chugging along in his "chopped" 1934 Chevy. It was a junk heap with a cardboard "window" on the driver's side. McKeechern had cut a three-by-three-inch flap in the cardboard, which he lifted when turning left. You could see his evil eyes peering out just before he went around corners. When the flap was down, however, he was unaware of things happening on the left side of the car. As luck would have it, that's where I was standing with a huge snowball in my hand—thinking very funny and terribly unwise thoughts.

If I could just go back to that day and counsel myself, I would say, *Don't do it, Jim! You could lose your sweet life right here. McKeechern will tear your tongue out if you hit him with that snowball. Just put it down and go quietly to your afternoon class. Please, son! If you lose, I lose!* Unfortunately, no such advice wafted to my ears that day, and I didn't have the sense to realize my danger. I heaved the snowball in the upper atmosphere with all my might. It came down just as McKeechern drove by and, unbelievably, went through the flap in his cardboard window. The missile obviously hit him squarely in the face, because his Chevy wobbled all over the road. It bounced over the curb and came to a stop just short of the school building.

Killer exploded from the front seat, ready to rip

someone (me!) to shreds. I'll never forget the sight. There was snow all over his face and little jets of steam were curling from his head. My whole life passed in front of my eyes as I faded into the crowd. *So young!* I thought.

> *I still have recurring nightmares about the event all these years later.*

The only thing that saved me on this snowy day was McKeechern's inability to identify me. No one told him I had thrown the snowball, and believe me, I didn't volunteer. I escaped unscathed, although that brush with destiny must have made a great impact on me emotionally. I still have recurring nightmares about the event all these years later. In my dreams, the chimes ring and I go to open the front door. There stands McKeechern with a shotgun. And he still has snow on his face. (If you read this story, Killer, I do hope we can be friends. We were only kids, you know? No offense, right? Howsa car?)

THE LIFELONG QUEST FOR POWER

Why have I described the power struggles of the adolescent years in this detail? What does that turbulent period have to do with the critical decade and beyond? Well, it is highly relevant to the issues at hand and figures prominently in your own future. As I have indicated, the quest for power is a lifelong passion for many people. It takes different forms in the adult years, but the emotional wellspring is the same. Most of us want to run things. Even the desire for money is a function of this longing for control and influence. Why? Because those with the most money are perceived as being the most powerful.

Just how important is raw power in your own motivational system? Will it shape your choice of a career? Do you hope to be a doctor, lawyer, military officer, or politician because these professions represent influence in the culture? Are you determined to make a name for yourself? Do you want people to say when you pass, "There goes a great person"? Do you hope they'll want your autograph and your photograph? Is your purpose in living to be found in these symbols of significance?

If so, your ladder is leaning against the wrong wall. But let me hasten to clarify. God has given you talent, and He wants you to use it productively. You should set your goals high and direct your energies toward achieving them. Train your mind. Develop your skills. Discipline your appetites. Prepare for the future. Work hard. Go for it! You can't steal second with one foot on first.

But before you set out to make your mark, you should ask yourself, "For whom will this be done?" If you seek power so you can be powerful, you're on the wrong track. If you crave fame so you can be famous, the journey will be disappointing. If you desire influence so you can be influential, you're making a big mistake. This is what the Lord says about these trappings of success: "Let not the wise man glory in his wisdom, neither let the mighty man glory in his might, let not the rich man glory in his riches" (Jer. 9:23 KJV). What then should we glory in? The apostle Paul provides the answer: "So whether you eat or drink or whatever you do, do it all for the glory of God" (1 Cor. 10:31).

If you seek power so you can be powerful, you're on the wrong track.

That's very clear, isn't it? Our purposes are not our own. They are His. Thus, the choice of an occupation and "whatever you do" is to be motivated by your service to the kingdom of God. That is the only thing that carries eternal significance. Nothing else will satisfy. Everything else is going to burn.

I have lived long enough to see some of my early dreams of glory come unstitched. One of them began shortly after I graduated from high school and went off to college. I arrived on campus several days before classes started and walked around looking at the place that would be my home for the next four years. I was like a tourist on holiday.

Of greatest interest to me that morning was the trophy case standing in the main administration building. There behind the glass were the glitzy symbols of past athletic victories. Basketball, track, and baseball were well represented there. Then I saw it. Standing majestically at the center of the case was the perpetual tennis trophy. It was about two feet tall and had a shiny little man on top. Engraved on the shaft were the names of all the collegiate tennis champions back to 1947. Every one of those heroes was burned into my memory. I could name most of them today.

As I stood there before that historic trophy, I said to myself, *Someday! Some fine day I'm going to add my name to that list of legends.* I set my jaw and determined to show the world.

As strange as it may seem today, becoming our college tennis champ was my highest goal in living at that time. Nothing could have mattered more to me. Tennis had been my passion in high school.

I had played six days a week and eleven months per year. When I graduated and headed for college, it was with the intention of riding this sport into the record books.

Well, I did have a certain amount of success with my tennis career. I lettered all four years, captained the team as a senior, and yes, got my name inscribed on the big trophy. In fact, I did it twice during each of my last two seasons. I left the college with the satisfaction of knowing that future generations of freshmen would stand at the display case and read my name in admiration. Someday they might be great like me.

WHERE'S THAT TROPHY NOW?

Alas, about fifteen years later a friend had reason to visit the college I attended. He was dumping something in the trash behind the administration building, and what do you suppose he found? Yep, there among the garbage and debris was the perpetual tennis trophy! The athletic department had actually thrown it away! What a blow! There I was, a legend in my own time, and who cared? Some universities retire the jersey numbers of their greatest athletes. My school didn't retire my number. They retired my memory!

The friend, Dr. Wil Spaite, who had been one of my teammates in college, took the tennis trophy home and cleaned it up. He put a new shiny man on the top and bought a new base for it. Then he gave it to me to commemorate our "prime," which everyone appeared to have forgotten. That trophy stands in my office today. I'll show it to you if you come by for a visit. My name is on it twice. You'll be impressed. It was a big deal at the time. Honest.

This brief encounter with fame has taught me a valuable lesson about success and achievement. Pay attention now, because this could be on the mid-term: IF YOU LIVE LONG ENOUGH, LIFE WILL TRASH YOUR TROPHIES, TOO. I don't care how important something seems at the time; if it is an end in itself, the passage of time will render it old and tarnished. Who cares today that Zachary Taylor or William

My school didn't retire my number. They retired my memory!

Henry Harrison won their elections for president of the United States? Can you name three U. S. senators in the year 1933? Probably not, and who cares anyway? What difference did it make that the Brooklyn Dodgers defeated the Yankees in the 1955 World Series? The hero of that series, Sandy Amoros, made a game-saving catch that a nation cheered, but he was soon penniless, forgotten, and living on the streets.[3]

John Gilbert was the biggest romantic male movie star of the 1920s. He was by far the highest-paid actor in Hollywood, and his name was given top billing in every movie in which he starred. Almost everyone in the country knew his name. But within two years, no studio would hire him. Gilbert died in 1936 from a heart attack brought on by alcohol and drug abuse. He was just thirty-six years old.[4] Have you ever heard of him? I doubt it. My point is that even the most awesome triumphs lose their sizzle in time.

Even the most awesome triumphs lose their sizzle in time.

Let me bring the matter closer to home. In November 1974, the University of Southern California's football team played its historic rival, Notre Dame, at the Coliseum in Los Angeles. It was one of the most exciting games in history, especially for USC fans. I attended graduate school at USC, and I still get very jazzed about its football games. And there are very few pleasures more gratifying for me than beating the socks off Notre Dame! (Supporters of the Irish will just have to forgive me.)

Well, that November day in '74 produced one of the greatest football games of all times. Notre Dame ripped through the Trojans in the first half, leading 24-6 at halftime. I don't know what Coach John McKay said to his team in the locker room, but something set USC on fire. They were an entirely different club in the second half. A tailback named Anthony (A. D.) Davis took the opening kickoff eighty-five yards for a touchdown. That started one of the most unbelievable comebacks in the history of the series. By the final gun, A. D. had scored four touchdowns, and USC had put 54 points on the board.

I was watching the game on television that afternoon. There I was in my study, cheering and screaming as though I were surrounded by 100,000 fans in the Coliseum. I never sat down through the second half! It was some kind of day.

A. D. Davis was the hero of the game, of course. He was on talk shows, and his picture was on virtually every sports page in the country the next morning. He had his day in the sun, to be sure. Football fans everywhere were talking about Anthony and his four explosive touchdowns.

Well, many years went by, and USC was again engaged in another make-or-break football game. This time the opponent was UCLA, and the winner would be going to the Rose Bowl on January 1, 1990. I was on the sidelines that day as the Trojans pulled off another miracle and scored a last-minute touchdown to win. The athletic director at that time, Mike McGee, is a friend of mine, and he invited me into the locker room after the game. It was another wonderful victory in the history of USC football.

The two heroes of the day, Rodney Peete and Eric Afhaulter, were hoisted to the shoulders of their teammates, and everyone was singing the Trojan fight song. It was a fine experience just being there.

Then I was distracted momentarily and looked to my left. There in the shadows was A. D. Davis, the superstar of 1974. He was watching the hullabaloo from the sidelines. I don't mean to be disrespectful to him because it happens to all of us, but A. D. didn't look like the finely tuned athlete I remembered from the past. He had put on some weight and had acquired a little belly that wasn't there in his prime. Here was "Mr. Yesterday," watching the new whiz kids and probably remembering what it was like to be in the spotlight. But his time on center stage had come and gone, and now—what did it really matter?

SUCCESS, TOO, WILL FADE

That's the way the system works. Your successes will fade from memory, too. That doesn't mean you shouldn't try to achieve them. But it should lead you to ask, Why are they important to me? Are my trophies for me, or are they for Him? Those are critical questions that every believer is obligated to answer.

Permit me one more illustration that relates not to sports but to the acquisition of political power. We've

seen that the desire for influence and control is basic
to the human personality, especially among men. But
how much satisfaction does it bring to those who
achieve it? I would not deny that authority is intoxi-
cating for some people and that they crave the perks
that go with it. Nevertheless, power is at best a tem-
porary phenomenon that eventually must be surren-
dered. That brings me to this final illustration.

Gary Bauer, president of the Family Research
Council in Washington, D. C., served for eight years
in the Reagan White House. He was chief domestic
policy adviser during the latter part of that era and
worked in a beautiful paneled office near the president. His boss was a man named Donald Regan,
chief of staff for the administration. Regan was one
tough customer! He was a no-nonsense executive
who intimidated those who worked for him. It was a
fearful thing to be called into his office for a repri-
mand. Regan was at the pinnacle of world power,
representing the president and sharing his awesome
authority.

One day, Gary was sick with the flu and stayed
home in bed. He was watching CNN on television
and learned, unbelievably, that Don Regan had been
summarily fired by President Reagan. As it was later
learned, Mr. Regan had made the mistake of irritat-
ing Nancy Reagan, and she saw to it that he was

canned. Recognizing that everything was up for grabs, Gary got out of bed despite a 102-degree fever and drove to Washington. He parked his car and walked through the main gate of the White House. There he met Don Regan coming out the front entrance. Incredibly, he was carrying his own boxes. He had been one of the most powerful men in the world two hours earlier; now he didn't even have anyone to help him clean out his office. Regan had been watching the same CNN broadcast that Gary had seen. That's how he learned he had been fired. Suddenly, it was over. He was a has-been. So much for the permanence and reliability of power!

I'm sure you see the relevance of these examples to your life, but let me leave no doubt. If the triumphs of the world's superstars and powerbrokers so quickly turn to dust, how much less significant will be the modest achievements you and I will be likely to garner? If our successes are simply ends in themselves, are they worth the investment of our years? Do they justify our brief tenure on this mortal soil? Is that all there is to a fire? I believe most passionately that it is not!

6 Sound Advice from a Dying King

IT IS REPORTED IN 1 CHRONICLES 28, WHEN King David had grown old and knew he was dying that he called together his officials, military leaders, business managers, and "mighty men" to hear his final words. In the assembly that day was his son Solomon, whom God had designated to succeed David as king.

The advice David gave that day was of great significance, not only for Solomon but also for you and me. A person doesn't waste words when the death angel hovers nearby. Picture the scene, then, as the old man offers his last thoughts to his beloved son who would carry on his legacy. This is what David said, probably with strong feeling and a shaky voice:

"And thou, Solomon my son, know thou the God of thy father, and serve him with a perfect heart and with a willing mind: for the LORD searcheth all

41

hearts, and understandeth all the imaginations of the thoughts: if thou seek him, he will be found of thee; but if thou forsake him, he will cast thee off forever" (1 Chron. 28:9 KJV).

A lifetime of wisdom was packed into that brief statement. Notice first that David advised Solomon to "know" God. He didn't say "know about God." I know about Abraham Lincoln, but I've never met him. David wanted Solomon to be acquainted personally with the God of Israel, whom he had tried to serve with a willing mind.

Then the king laid before his son the fundamental issue facing every person who ever lived. He said, "If thou seek him, he will be found of thee; but if thou forsake him, he will cast thee off forever." If I had a thousand years to consider a final message for my son or daughter, I couldn't improve on these last words of David.

It is also my best advice to you as we conclude this discussion of purposes and goals. Whatever else you set out to do, begin by getting to know God and seeking His will in your life. If you do that, you *will* find Him. He *will* lead you. He *will* bless you. What a wonderful promise! But it is conditional. If you turn your back on the Lord, He will cast you off forever.

The young prince went on to become perhaps the richest, most famous, and most glamorous king in the history of the world. He received twenty-five tons of gold every year (at today's value that is $308 million). The Scripture says, "King Solomon was greater in riches and wisdom than all the other kings of the earth. All the kings of the earth sought audience with Solomon to hear the wisdom God had put in his heart. Year after year, everyone who came brought a gift—articles of silver and gold, and robes, weapons and spices, and horses and mules.

Solomon had four thousand stalls for horses and chariots, and twelve thousand horses, which he kept in the chariot cities and also with him in Jerusalem. He ruled over all the kings from the River to the land of the Philistines, as far as the border of Egypt. The king made silver as common in Jerusalem as stones, and cedar as plentiful as sycamore-fig trees in the foothills. Solomon's horses were imported from Egypt and from other countries" (2 Chron. 9:22–31).

NOW, THAT'S POWER!

That, ladies and gentlemen, is known as *power!* Indeed, Solomon may have been the most powerful and respected man of all times. No good thing was withheld from him. For the purposes of our discussion, wouldn't it be helpful to know how he felt about the abundance he enjoyed? Well, fortunately, that information is available to us. Solomon wrote his innermost thoughts and recorded them in a book we know today as Ecclesiastes. The following excerpts are extremely important to understanding the point I have tried to make. Please read them carefully!

I undertook great projects: I built houses for myself and planted vineyards. I made gardens and parks and planted all kinds of fruit trees in them. I made reservoirs to water groves of flourishing trees. I bought male and female slaves and had other slaves who were born in my house. I owned more herds and flocks than anyone in Jerusalem before me. I amassed silver and gold for myself, and the treasure of kings and provinces. I acquired men and women singers, and a harem as well—the delights of the heart of man. I became greater by far than anyone in Jerusalem before me. In all this my wisdom stayed with me.

I denied myself nothing my eyes desired; I refused my heart no pleasure. My heart took delight in all my work, and this was the reward for all my labor. Yet when I surveyed all that my hands had done and what I had toiled to achieve, everything was meaningless, a chasing after the wind, nothing was gained under the sun. . . .

So I hated life, because the work that is done under the sun was grievous to me. All of it is meaningless, a chasing after the wind. I hated all the things I had toiled for under the sun, because I must leave them to the one who comes after me. And who knows whether he will be a wise man or a fool? Yet he will have control over all the work into which I have poured my effort and skill under the sun. This too is meaningless. (Eccles. 2:4–11, 17–19)

What an incredible passage of Scripture this is, coming straight from the heart of an old man who had become disillusioned with life! It does not tell the entire story, however. Solomon failed to mention that he had strayed from the advice of his father and fell

> *A person doesn't waste words when the death angel hovers nearby.*

into grievous sin. God had specifically warned the children of Israel not to marry women from nations that worshiped idols and false gods. But Solomon willfully disobeyed this commandment and took hundreds of these foreigners to be his wives and concubines. The scripture then tells where that defiance led.

As Solomon grew old, his wives turned his heart after other gods, and his heart was not fully devoted to the Lord his God, as the heart of David his father had been. He followed Ashtoreth the goddess of the Sidonians, and Molech the detestable god of the Ammonites. So

Solomon did evil in the eyes of the Lord; he did not follow the Lord completely, as David his father had done. (1 Kings 11:4–6)

Now we know why Solomon was so depressed in the latter years of his life. He had betrayed the God of his father, David. He had bowed before idols used by pagan nations for the most unthinkable wickedness, including orgies and the sacrifice of innocent children. Yet Solomon, who had conversed with God and received every good gift from His hand, persisted in worshiping these evil symbols. Then he enticed the people of Israel to do likewise. Consequently, Solomon had lost all meaning in life, which explains his boredom with his riches. God's hand was no longer on him.

The lesson for the rest of us is clear. If we ignore the Lord and violate His commandments, there will be no meaning for us, either. The temporal things of this world, even vast riches and power, will not deliver the satisfaction they advertise! There must be something more substantial on which to base one's values, purposes, and goals. And of course there is. Jesus said it succinctly: "But seek ye *first* the kingdom of God, and his righteousness; and all these things shall be added unto you" (Matt. 6:33 KJV, emphasis mine).

I rest my case.

Notes

1. "Eleanor Rigby," The Beatles, © 1966 Capitol Records, MacLen Music—EMI/ Blackwood (ASCAP).

2. Ron and Judy Blue, *Money Matters for Parents and Their Kids* (Nashville: Thomas Nelson, 1988), 46.

3. Brendan C. Boyd and Fred C. Harris, *The Great American Baseball Card Flipping, Trading, and Bubble Gum Book,* (NY: Ticknor & Fields, 1991).

4. *Hollywood,* "Episode 12: Star Treatment," Thames Television Network, London, England, 1980.

About the Author

DR. JAMES DOBSON is founder and president of Focus on the Family, a non-profit evangelical organization dedicated to the preservation of the home. He is recognized as one of America's foremost authorities on the family and is the author of numerous books, including *The New Dare to Discipline, The Strong-Willed Child, When God Doesn't Make Sense, Love Must Be Tough, Straight Talk to Men, Parenting Isn't for Cowards,* and *Life on the Edge: A Young Adult's Guide to a Meaningful Future.* Dr. Dobson is a licensed psychologist in the state of California and a licensed marriage, family and child therapist in the state of Colorado. He was formerly an assistant professor of pediatrics at the University of Southern California School of Medicine. His international radio broadcast, *Focus on the Family,* is heard on more than four thousand stations worldwide. He and his wife, Shirley, are the parents of two young adult children, Ryan and Danae.

PORTIONS OF THIS SERIES OF BOOKS HAVE BEEN previously published in other books by James Dobson. The author is grateful to these publishers for permission to reprint from these volumes:

Thirty-eight Values to Live By, Word Publishing, 2000.

Life on the Edge: A Young Adult's Guide to a Meaningful Future, Word Publishing, 1995.

Dr. Dobson Answers Your Questions, Tyndale House Publishers, 1988.

Emotions: Can You Trust Them? Regal Books, 1984.

Hide or Seek, Fleming H. Revell Company, 1974, 1990.

Love for a Lifetime, Multnomah, 1987.

Love Must Be Tough, Word Publishing, 1983.

Parenting Isn't for Cowards, Word Publishing, 1987.

Preparing for Adolescence, Regal Books, 1980, 1989.

The Strong-Willed Child, Tyndale House Publishers, 1978.

Straight Talk to Men and Their Wives, Word Publishing, 1980.

What Wives Wish Their Husbands Knew about Women, Tyndale House Publishers, 1975.

When God Doesn't Make Sense, Tyndale House Publishers, 1993.

dditional books in the *Life on the Edge* Series:

Adapted from the best-selling book, *Life on the Edge*, these
seven pocket-sized booklets offer insight and advice for a
generation searching for significance. Additional books in
this series cover such topics as:

emotions

love

money

compatibility

God's will

parents

life's ironies

W WORD PUBLISHING

www.wordpublishing.com